KILLER
WHALES

Printed in China
First editon: 99   00   01   02   03   9   8   7   6   5
Revised edition: 01   02   03   04   05   5   4   3   2   1
Library of Congress Cataloging-in-Publication Data available

ISBN 0-89658-545-X

Distributed in Canada by Raincoast Books, 9050 Shaughnessy Street, Vancouver, B.C. V6P 6E5

Published by Voyageur Press, Inc.
123 North Second Street, P.O. Box 338, Stillwater, MN 55082 U.S.A.
651-430-2210, fax 651-430-2211
books@voyageurpress.com
www.voyageurpress.com

Educators, fundraisers, premium and gift buyers, publicists, and marketing managers:
Looking for creative products and new sales ideas? Voyageur Press books are available at special discounts when purchased in quantities, and special editions can be created to your specifications. For details contact the marketing department at 800-888-9653.

Photographs copyright © 2001 by

Front Cover © Fred Felleman (Tony Stone Images)
Back Cover © David E Myers (Tony Stone Images)
Page 1 © Michael Nolan (Marine Mammal Images)
Page 4 © Graeme Ellis
Page 6 © D Parer & E Parer-Cook (Ardea)
Page 8 © Kelley Balcomb-Bartok
Page 9 © Flip Nicklin (Minden Pictures)
Page 10 © Eda Rogers (Marine Mammal Images)
Page 12 © Graeme Ellis
Page 13 © Graeme Ellis
Page 14 © Marc Webber (Planet Earth Pictures)
Page 17 © Pete Atkinson (Planet Earth Pictures)
Page 18 © Kelley Balcomb-Bartok
Page 20 © Kelley Balcomb-Bartok
Page 23 © Jim Boran & Sara Heimlich
Page 24 © Kelley Balcomb-Bartok
Page 25 Top © Jim Boran & Sara Heimlich
Page 25 Bottom © Kelley Balcomb-Bartok
Page 26 © Heather Angel
Page 29 © Graeme Ellis
Page 30 © Kelley Balcomb-Bartok
Page 33 © Duncan Murrell (Planet Earth Pictures)
Page 34 © Kelley Balcomb-Bartok
Page 37 © Hanne Strager
Page 38 © Jeff Foott (Bruce Coleman Collection)

Page 41 Top © Pieter Folkens (Planet Earth Pictures)
Page 41 Bottom © Kelley Balcomb-Bartok
Page 42 © D Parer & E Parer-Cook (Ardea)
Page 44 © Heather Angel
Page 46 © Duncan Murrell (Planet Earth Pictures)
Page 47 © Kelley Balcomb-Bartok
Page 49 © Pieter Folkens (Marine Mammal Images)
Page 50 © Kelley Balcomb-Bartok
Page 52 © Graeme Ellis
Page 53 © Pieter Folkens (Planet Earth Pictures)
Page 54 © Graeme Ellis
Page 55 © Francois Gohier (Ardea)
Page 56 Top Left © Ned Middleton (Planet Earth Pictures)
Page 56 Top Right © Peter Johnson (NHPA)
Page 57 © Flip Nicklin (Minden Pictures)
Page 58 © Jeff Foott (Bruce Coleman Collection)
Page 61 © Jim Boran & Sara Heimlich
Page 63 © James D Watt (Planet Earth Pictures)
Page 64 © Kelley Balcomb-Bartok
Page 66 Top © Flip Nicklin (Minden Pictures)
Page 66 Bottom © Flip Nicklin (Minden Pictures)
Page 67 © Kelley Balcomb-Bartok
Page 69 © Jim Boran & Sara Heimlich
Page 70 © Mark Carwardine (Biotica)

UPDATED EDITION

KILLER
WHALES

Sara Heimlich & James Boran

WORLDLIFE
LIBRARY

Voyageur Press

Contents

Killer Whales

Long ago, in what is now southeastern Alaska, a land rich in fish and fowl and furred creatures, Natsihlane, a skilled Tlingit Indian woodsman, went hunting with his brothers-in-law. All but the youngest were jealous of Natsihlane. They abandoned Natsihlane on a distant island, while the youngest despaired.

Natsihlane felt very sad and wondered if he would ever see his wife again. That night, a seagull came to him and flew with him to the home of the sea lions. Their chief put Natsihlane inside an inflated sea-lion stomach, laid it in the water, and instructed him to think hard about the beach near his village. He soon found himself there and began to plan revenge on his brothers-in-law.

He got different pieces of wood and began to whittle blackfish. He tried spruce, then red cedar, then hemlock, painting each in stripes of different colors. But no amount of singing or shouting would bring them alive.

Finally, he carefully carved fine yellow cedar into eight large and small blackfish. He painted each with a white band across the head and a white circle on the dorsal fin. He sang his most powerful songs for them, commanding them to go. They swam about, and soon the bay was full of spray from their spouting and playing.

After many days, Natsihlane saw his brothers-in-laws' canoe far out at sea. He commanded the blackfish to destroy all but the youngest. They swam out and around and around the canoe. The men and the craft disappeared, but two blackfish saved the youngest brother-in-law and carried him towards the shore.

Natsihlane called the blackfish to him and said: 'When I made you I did not intend that you should kill human beings. I made you to get revenge on my brothers-in-law. Hereafter you shall not harm human beings but help them when they are in trouble. Now go.' And they swam out to sea, the first killer whales in the world.

Adapted from a Tlingit Indian folktale.

Killer whales, the most dramatic and the largest of the dolphins, feature in legends from all parts of the globe. The mythological powers attributed to them and many other large mammals reflect the active human imagination, sparked by the impressive qualities of the living animals.

As researchers who have had 17 years of privileged familiarity with a group of killer whales, we recall our first impressions vividly: a white eye patch and gray dorsal saddle the only visible clues of a large being in the depths of velvety-green waters; a dark body discernible only just before breaking the surface with a blow; the swoop of a back and the immensity of a dorsal fin; the grace of a roll through the water; the flip of a wide tail at the end of a breathing sequence; the sweep of exhaled breath drifting across your face; a white belly and black back suspended against a blue sky during an exuberant, high, backwards jump.

Orcinus orca emerges from the deep.

Each time we see killer whales, we are reminded how strange and remarkable it is that these creatures, which move with such ease through the three-dimensional and highly dynamic marine world, are mammals like us; that while we share much of the same basic anatomy and both breathe air, they are supremely adapted to a watery environment which would, without artificial support, kill us terrestrial mammals.

Known by early whalers as 'whale killers', killer whales once had a reputation as voracious predators killing on a whim; stories of their attacks on boats and people fuelled the aura of menace. Concentrated efforts to understand them began only after the first killer whale capture in the early 1960s. Since then, as details of their lives in captivity and in the wild have been revealed, many long-held misconceptions about killer whales, harbored over centuries, have been replaced with evidence of an astoundingly complex creature. Reflecting changing attitudes, the common name for the species is becoming 'orca', which derives from the scientific name, *Orcinus orca*.

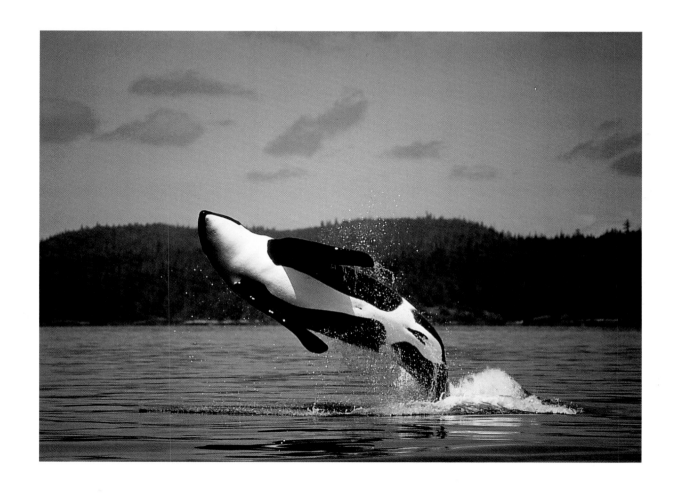

*Exuberant leaps are common and add to the drama which
has inspired generations of story-tellers, poets and artists. Mundane explanations
for leaping have included to remove parasites and to communicate with distant whales,
but the high-energy antics also seem to be done just for the fun of it!*

Looking into the eye of a killer whale, an oceanic mammal. All whales have excellent eyesight, both above and below the water, which is important when sonar echolocation is not being used, for example when hunting silently. The white 'eye-spot' above the killer whales' eye may be used by other whales to help see body orientation when traveling in murky waters.

Most of our knowledge of killer whales comes from long-term studies in Washington State and British Columbia – the North American Pacific Northwest. The first observations, begun in 1971 by scientists of the Canadian Pacific Biological Station, were planned to provide a population estimate for killer whales in Canada. Capture operations had been ongoing since the mid 1960s. In order to decide whether they should be continued, the Canadian government wanted to know how many killer whales were left.

After an initial summer-long survey along northeastern Vancouver Island, the researchers returned the following year and recognized some of the same individual killer whales by distinctive scars and marks on their dorsal fins and backs. They decided to create a photographic catalog of individuals as a tool for counting the population. A careful examination and comparison of photographs, collected in hundreds of hours of observation at sea, provided a count of killer whales frequenting the inland waters off eastern Vancouver Island.

The most exciting discovery in those early days was that these killer whales lived in three different groups, which never interacted with one another. The group regularly found off northeastern Vancouver Island was named the northern resident community. Another group consistently ranged off southeastern Vancouver Island and was called the southern resident community. These two communities never crossed the central region of Vancouver Island into each others' territories. However, a third, smaller group of killer whales sporadically roamed throughout both precincts, and were referred to as the transient community. Another discrete community, termed the 'offshore' community has been discovered off west Vancouver Island.

Alarmingly, nearly all the live captures for display in aquariums were discovered to have been of whales taken from the southern resident community. Forty-eight whales had been removed from the southern resident population in the 1960s and the 1970s, and only 80 remained by 1976. It was clear that captures could no longer be allowed from this community.

Dedicated research on killer whales began in 1976 when the government of the United States decided to conduct a study to compare the Canadian research results with killer whale observations from adjacent US waters. A host of researchers have come and gone since then, monitoring the population in the region and keeping a diversity of studies alive. Long-term research sites have also sprung up in Scandinavia, Argentina and elsewhere. Their findings have been similar, and have permitted a more global understanding of how killer whales live.

We now recognize that killer whales have specialized feeding strategies, developed to exploit the prominent food resource at hand. Although named 'residents' and 'transients' the two types of killer whales are distinct more because of their feeding specializations rather than their residency patterns. 'Residents' and 'transients' are not only different in feeding strategies, but also group size and social structures, and are actually distinct genetic races which may be evolving into separate species. To find such striking differences between two groups of the same species exploiting the same habitat is unusual.

Tail flukes are adaptations to a water habitat.

We now accept that killer whales have a long lifespan, equivalent to that of humans, and live in highly social, cooperative groups, organized through complex vocal repertoires distinct to each group. In captivity, they have surprised us with their ability to learn dialects from other whales and have proved to be inquisitive, often gentle, and easily trained.

Whether free or captive, killer whales continue to evoke the interest of scientists and public alike. Since the mid 1970s, the attention they have received has increased dramatically. Each investigation, whether experimental or observational, enriches our understanding of these unique marine mammals.

A family cluster completely at ease with their marine world.
The close ties of a killer whale pod lead to lifelong associations which contribute
to the complex, cooperative behaviors needed to make a living in the sea.

Oceanic Mammals

We had been following killer whales through the lustrous afternoon; a lazy meandering while they fished, with long pauses for deep dives. Everything was still and relaxed. Without warning, Merlin, a large male, rose vertically through the surface, almost rubbing against the boat. First the blunt snout, then the rounded black head, scattering diamond-bright water droplets, then the white patch above the eye, and then the eye itself, brown and intent. In that instant, we realised how truly well-adapted whales and dolphins are for their marine environment. While we clung to the boat, dependent on it for our survival in an environment alien to our land-adapted anatomy, the killer whale moved easily and with confidence. Yet we were both warm-blooded, milk-producing, air-breathing mammals, looking eye-to-eye. And, like us, killer whales have risen to the top of the food chain, able to survive in a variety of habitats.

Personal Diary, August

'Bufeo de mascarilla', 'Spaekhuggare', 'Sadshi', 'Mesungesak', 'Kosatka', 'Innuata': local names for killer whales in Spain, Sweden, Japan, Alaska, Russia and Korea, and just a few of the hundreds found around the world, reflect the mammals' ability to live in every ocean and to thrive in a wide range of habitats. From prehistoric rock paintings to modern ship-based censuses, killer whales have been reported from nearly every corner of the globe. Although killer whales are most common over the continental shelf in cooler seas near the North and South Poles, very little is known of their movements on a global scale and there is no reliable estimate of the world population.

Clusters of killer whales were commonly encountered by whalers across the entire North Atlantic. Although no longer common in some of the areas they once inhabited, killer whales still roam the coasts of North Africa and continental Europe and, infrequently, into the Mediterranean. They are regular visitors to British and Irish waters between April and September, particularly along the Atlantic seaboard, the Western Isles and in the North Sea. As in Norwegian and Icelandic waters, they are probably following the movements of spawning Atlantic salmon and herring.

In the eastern Pacific, Pre-Christian peoples from the Chukchi Sea to the equator commonly encountered killer whales. The Nasca of Peru worshipped killer whales and built temples dedicated to them. Killer whales are now most commonly found along the coasts of the Alaskan Peninsula, Prince William Sound in the Gulf of Alaska, Georges Strait and around Vancouver Island in British Columbia, and Puget Sound, Washington State; this Northwest Coast population is considered one of the world's most dense. They also occur off the coasts of Oregon, California, Baja California and the Gulf of California, Mexico, and between Cabo San Lucas and the Galapagos Islands off South America. Although there is a concentration off Japan, there is little evidence that killer whales were ever common in the mid-oceanic Pacific.

One of the best indications of the current distribution of killer whale concentrations is the location where field studies are being conducted. In addition to the Pacific Northwest, there are projects in southern Alaska, Argentina, Norway, Iceland, and Marion Island and the Crozet Islands in the Indian Ocean. According to recent photographic censuses, 335 individuals have been identified in the Pacific Northwest, 232 in Prince William Sound, Alaska, 26 in Argentina, around 350 in Norway, 143 in Iceland and 76 in the Crozet Islands and over 45 in U.K. waters. Appearance, behavior and some biological traits differ in some of these populations indicating long-term adaptations to the local environment.

These populations may have originated from larger aggregations ranging the wider ocean basins. Killer whales observed at sea are reported in groups of 200-300, yet remain subdivided into smaller clusters spaced from several hundred yards to half a mile apart. Although it has been suggested that there is one population in the Pacific, cruising a territory which covers the vast expanse of ocean between Asia and America and between the two poles, it is more plausible that there are clumped populations which roam through specific ranges, their movements governed by seasonal changes in the environment and prey.

The coastal pockets with localized killer whale populations typically possess abundant marine life, especially fish. The passage of many generations is required for killer whale communities to become established in such coastal areas: a slow behavioral and social adaptation to abundant local resources, reflecting long-standing forces affecting killer whale evolution.

The ancestors of all whales and dolphins were extinct land mammals, which also gave rise to modern cows, horses, sheep and ungulates. Millions of years ago, they lived at the edge of a

Saddle patch pattern and dorsal fin shape are unique to
each individual killer whale, just as hair color and face shape are unique
to every human. These open hook-shaped patches are common to many of the
resident killer whales of Washington and British Columbia, but are
rare in many other killer whale populations.

great inland sea, long before the earth's continents shifted into the positions they now hold. Over time and for unknown reasons, their descendants gradually moved into the sea, their bodies adapting for survival in an alien environment. Primitive whales first appeared around 50-60 million years ago. Most of the modern types had appeared by 20 million years ago.

Class, Order, Family, Genus, Species. These are the five basic levels which make up a scientific address for all organisms on Earth. Like a postal address, organized in order of country, area of postal code, city, street and number, each level in the hierarchy serves to clarify the exact position of an organism in the general scheme of life. In this classification system, each division is based on commonly held characteristics, beginning with the most general and ending with the most specific. The basic two-part scientific name for each organism combines its genus and species names and reflects its place and connections to other organisms. Killer whales are scientifically known as *Orcinus orca*: their genus name meaning 'belonging to the realms of the dead', and their species name a derivative of Orcus, an ogre and Roman god of the underworld. Whales and dolphins belong to the class Mammalia, Order Cetacea. They are collectively known as cetaceans and are divided into two suborders: those with teeth, called the Odontoceti, and those with baleen, called the Mysticeti.

The Odontoceti are subdivided into families by tooth type, skull structure and other anatomical characteristics. The Delphinidae are just one of several toothed cetacean families and embrace all dolphins. Killer whales, *Orcinus orca*, are anatomically similar to smaller dolphins and have been placed in this family. Yet their larger size, round head, blunt 'beak' and fewer teeth are characteristics shared with other globe-headed species, like pilot whales. This has caused debate about their classification, with some taxonomists arguing they should belong to a group called the Orcininae or Globicephalinae.

The Delphinidae originated around 11 million years ago. Killer whales are one of the oldest delphinid types and branched off very early from the main evolutionary group. Through time, delphinids underwent refinements on a basic type, each genera developing specialized adaptations, such as more teeth, longer or shorter jaws, unique coloration, feeding specializations. Killer whales, compared to other delphinids, have fewer modifications to the general plan and principally specialized a large body size to exploit large prey.

The killer whale tuxedo comes in only one model worldwide and does not change during an individual's life. The pattern is considered to be a very basic form of counter-shading, dark above and light below, thought to have originally evolved as a form of camouflage to avoid predation. The boldness of the killer whales' design may be due to their role as one of the top marine predators.

Killer whales cannot be confused with any other species, anywhere in the world. Their large size, robust shape, tall dorsal fins, oval flippers, and striking coloration are very characteristic and immediately recognizable. Females generally attain a length of 7 1/2 yards (7 m) and can weigh up to 6835 lbs (3100 kg). Males grow longer, up to 9 yds (8 m) and 8820 lbs (4000 kg). Calves are born measuring about 2 1/2 yds (2.2 m) long and weighing around 400 lbs (180 kg).

Killer whales have proportionately higher dorsal fins than other dolphins, from one-tenth to one-fifth of the total body length. The dorsal fins of males can grow up to 2 yards (1.8 m) in height and stand more than twice as high as those of adult females. The height of the dorsal fin is a useful way to distinguish adult males, but as it doesn't begin to grow until around age 10 and takes at least another seven years to reach its full height, distinguishing between subadult males and adult females is difficult.

The uniquely shaped, paddle-like pectoral flippers are also proportionately larger than other dolphins' and contrast with the sickle-shaped flippers of most delphinids. They lie about one quarter of the distance from the snout to the flukes. In males, flippers may reach 2 yds (2 m); about 20 per cent of the body length; the flippers in females reach 11-13 per cent.

Many dolphins and porpoises have complex pigmentation patterns, yet killer whales wear a tidy black and white tuxedo affair. This simple counter-shading is believed to be the most generalized and probably also the most primitive within the dolphin family.

The white shirt-front extends from the lower jaw down to the genital region, the dark coat wrapping around the flippers to lie slightly open over the belly, revealing the genital area in a tri-section cut-away which closes smartly at the base of the tail. The cut of the dark coat is not quite identical in both sexes and the shape of the white genital field reveals the individual's sex. Males generally have a long, narrow middle section, while females sport a wide, almost circular shape. The faces of the flukes are also light-colored, as are the jaunty eye patches resting behind and above each eye. Wrapped just behind the dorsal fin is a gray patch in the shape of a horse saddle.

The basic pattern of a killer whale's suit at birth will remain fundamentally unchanged throughout its life. Very young calves are occasionally mistaken for porpoises: the saddle patch is often quite dark and the light-pigmented areas are commonly butterscotch or rusty-hued. But, before the end of the first year, the saddle dims to gray and the colors fade to white.

Variations in the pattern of the saddle are unique to individual killer whales. Researchers working on wild, free-ranging populations can recognize most individuals by the saddle's shape and pattern and confirm their notes with photographs of the individual they observe. Photographic identification is the fundamental tool for following an individual in its daily activities, throughout its life.

Each population bears slight variations to the general design. Killer whales hunted off Australia and New Zealand have been described as dark purplish-brown with ivory-hued areas. Killer whales in the Antarctic are smaller and distinctly more yellow than their northern relatives, and those off Mexico and in the Southern hemisphere have plain, featureless saddle patches, as do the transients of British Columbia and Washington State. Resident killer whales have complex saddle-patch features, and are significantly different from transients in the area.

Such variations in appearance come about from long-term isolation of killer whale communities: probably first isolated geographically, then reproductively, then genetically. The genetic distinctions separating the residents and transients living in the Pacific Northwest are thought to have begun evolving around 2 million years ago. The most likely scenario is that adaptations were developed for exploiting specific food types: fish versus other marine mammals. Consequently, the killer whale population concentrated in either the habitats of fish or of marine mammals. Over time, as separate communities developed, living different lives and no longer mating together, differences began to develop a genetic basis. This evolutionary process is what can lead to the formation of new species; while only one species of killer whale is still considered, residents and transients appear to be moving along the lines towards becoming separate species.

Further genetic variation also occurs between the two resident communities. These appear to have become genetically isolated around 40,000 years ago, when killer whales colonized the area as the glacial ice retreated. Separated by a tidal boundary which provides a natural barrier, the two communities have had little contact and remain genetically isolated.

The development of these variations is most likely based in the social fabric: a closed breeding system and a matriarchal structure which encourages strong family bonds and excludes outsiders.

These Pacific Northwest killer whales are genetically different to their Argentinean cousins, but look similar. Although the ocean is apparently an open territory without boundaries, killer whales often form localized populations exploiting especially abundant resources.

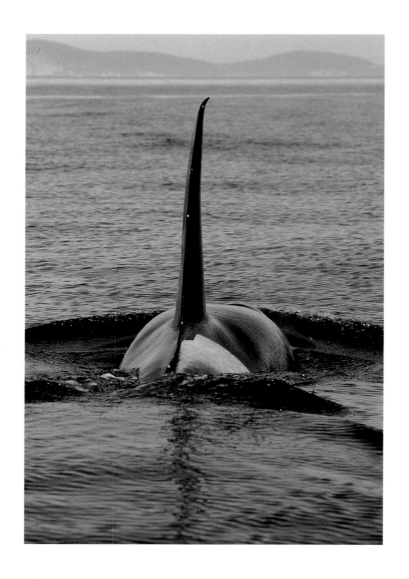

The towering dorsal fin takes several years to develop and indicates a fully adult male. Male killer whales are also recognizable by their great bulk and large, broad pectoral flippers.

Very young calves are born with an orange tint (see the lower photo), which eventually turns white. They grow rapidly in the first six months.

Family Ties

We were happy to see the end of the bad weather and get back onto the water. For weeks, we had been land-bound by black, storm-filled clouds and wild grey seas, watching from shore as the killer whales ploughed through the churning waters, oblivious to the screaming winds and nasty winter chill. We had been in the boat only a few minutes when young whales Blossom and Slick arrived, dallying in the calmer waters of the bay. Both were approaching maturity that year. Blossom had filled out and finally looked more like an adult female. We wondered if she would soon show up with her own calf. Slick's dorsal fin was slightly more elongated, but he still looked young. We knew it would be several more years before he gained the tall adult-male fin. We were fond of these older adolescents and could only hope they would live their maximum life span. On that fine day, watching them meander in the kelp beds, we knew Blossom could look forward to a very long life, but Slick's would be much shorter.

Personal Diary, February

Killer whales can lead very long lives and they have a complex life history. An astonishing story has unfolded through the long years of research on wild groups in the Pacific Northwest. At first some of the details seemed unbelievable. Yet, after 20 years of concentrated research, it is confirmed that killer whales exhibit some of the rarest traits in the mammalian plan. Humans are one of the few similar mammalian types.

As with humans, female killer whales live longer than males, up to 80 years, while males generally manage only 50-60 years. There is no single reason for this. Being a large male with all that body mass to feed and push through the water could simply be too stressful for a long life. Males certainly have greater food requirements to maintain their greater body size. They may also have a more stressful role in group protection. Perhaps even competition for access to females is more dangerous than has been observed. The road to sexual, physical and social maturity is a slow one, very much like our own. Until the age of about 10 years, there is little difference in how males and females develop.

Male killer whales reach sexual maturity at around age 15, in the midst of their adolescent growth. This is the time when the male dorsal fin begins to grow noticeably taller and when he starts to produce sperm. It does not mean, however, that he is socially ready, or permitted, to father calves. Social maturity occurs much later, when a male has become a fully grown adult and can pursue mates. In humans, the period between sexual maturity and social maturity is the transition period from childhood to adulthood, when the rules of the adult society are learned. The long period in killer whales is parallel. It is common in many mammals, exemplified by roving bands of 'bachelor' males, very similar to human teenagers.

Female killer whales mature sexually between 12 and 16 years of age and stop growing by the age of 18. Females in captivity ovulate throughout the year and exhibit 'spontaneous ovulation', meaning that they continue to ovulate even without the presence of a male. This is not common in mammals.

Calves take between 15 and 17 months to develop in the womb. So, theoretically, an adult female could give birth as frequently as every two years. But calves nurse for most of their first two years and this can influence the mother's next pregnancy. Weaning usually takes place toward the end of the second year, but can be prolonged if no other sibling appears.

An adult female is capable of producing around five calves over a 25 year period. Yet not all adult females produce calves like clockwork. The shortest observed gap between births is 2 years and the longest 12 years. If a calf dies at birth (and as many as 40 per cent do), a female may give birth again much sooner than normal.

Female killer whales appear to stop bearing calves in later life, rather like human females; an extremely uncommon trait in mammals. As most female mammals age, they decline in reproductive output but do not stop reproducing completely. However, many female killer whales in the Pacific Northwest have not had new calves for many years. Those who remain without a new calf for longer than 10 years are defined as 'post-reproductive'; living beyond their child-bearing years. Using a variety of age estimates, it appears that half of all killer whales older than 39 have stopped giving birth and by the age of 55, all females are post-reproductive. Although there is no direct proof that ovulation has ceased, biological studies on short-finned pilot whales, a closely related species, have shown a lack of ovulation in females over the age of 40. This strongly supports the existence of this later life stage in female killer whales. It has been estimated that one

This family group of Canadian killer whales is part of a multi-generational pod which consists of several other family groups. Each group or subpod generally travels separately from the rest of the pod. The female pictured to the right is accompanied by her two uncles.

Females and their offspring remain together throughout their lives. This close bond is strongest for male calves, who take longer to mature than females. As the mother has more calves, the older offspring will spend more time with older siblings, aunts, uncles and even grandmothers.

third of all adult females in the Pacific Northwest resident communities are post-reproductive.

These females may live 20 years or more after giving birth for the last time. The 20 to 30 year difference in male and female lifespans means the oldest members of any pod are most likely to be females. Mothers and even grandmothers will therefore often be alive throughout their sons' entire lives, but not their daughters'.

These life history parameters deeply affect the nature of killer whale society. Long periods of development and maturation provide increased exposure to the behaviors of elders and allows for the inter-generational transfer of skills. The longer lifespans of the females gives them greater experience and makes them the crucial element in the social structure.

The bulk of our knowledge about the social structure of killer whale groups is based on studies of resident communities in British Columbia and Washington State. Although the infrequent occurrence of transient killer whale groups has kept our knowledge about their social structure and group dynamics extremely limited, together, the two 'types' make an interesting story.

At the core of resident killer whale society, is the mother/calf pair; the structure of groups follows maternal lines. Bonds between adult females and offspring of both sexes are long-term and last well into adulthood, creating a basic unit of an adult female and her offspring, including adult sons. Typically, the unit will contain an older post-reproductive female, a mother with up to four calves of varying ages, and an adult male.

A 'pod' is made up of several such maternal sub-groups which are closely related. A rarity in mammals, neither males nor females leave the pod, but remain in the group into which they were born for their entire lifetime. Killer whale pods seem to be extended families of mothers, sisters, brothers, aunts, uncles, nieces, nephews and cousins. But there do not appear to be any fathers.

Calves are more likely to be products of matings between pods, rather than within pods. Since males and females in pods are closely related, and in any animal population it is preferable to avoid incest, it is unlikely that any breeding takes place within the pod. Although rarely observed, sex between killer whales has been between males and females from different pods. The end product of stable, non-breeding kin groups which are killer whale pods, is highly unique in mammals.

A community is simply several pods which live in the same area and frequently travel together. These larger communities are the breeding unit of associated pods. Genetic testing could tell us about the relatedness of individuals in a pod and in the larger community. Until such tests are carried out, we are left to combine speculation, observations from the field and theories of social biology to determine how this unique system could have developed.

Like most species of dolphins, killer whales are sexually promiscuous. Adult females are not only sexually active all year round, but also ovulate throughout the year. This means adult males have no guarantee which offspring might be theirs.

Having offspring, and investing time to guarantee their survival, is nature's way of passing genes on through time, and all creatures follow some sort of strategy for future representation of their genes. But, if a female killer whale is mating with many whales, who is to know which male fathered which calf?

Other male mammals herd females into harems, corralling them in jealously guarded territories and controlling access. Killer whales, living in the three-dimensional, boundary-less oceanic environment, have no such control.

A male killer whale can deal with this problem by mating with as many females as possible. This would flood the market, increasing his chances of producing offspring and having his genes represented in the next generation. But, since he cannot be guaranteed paternity, it is not cost effective for him to contribute paternal care to the offspring of any females he mates with. It is not in his best interests to invest time in calves which may be the offspring of other males.

Under these circumstances, an adult male is better off caring for the offspring of his sisters or his younger siblings, which he knows are kin. Although these calves are not passing on genes descending directly from him, they are carrying genes he has in common with his mother or sisters. Part of his genetic structure is guaranteed to go on. This is how an adult male killer whale can improve upon his 'reproductive success'.

Critical to the social bond holding pods and communities together are the older adult females who have passed their calf-bearing years. Alternatively called 'grannies', 'aunties' or 'allo-mothers', they have no dependent calves of their own but spend time, almost exclusively, with the calves of particular mothers. Looked at as game strategy, this has several important benefits.

Alaskan killer whales cluster around adult females, the matriarchs of killer whale societies. The females'
longer lifespans (on average they live 20 to 30 years longer than males) makes them the repository of long memories
of previous feeding successes, allowing them to guide the group through their wanderings.

Close bonds unite killer whale society. Synchronized behaviors,
like this double spyhop, may be practice to help the pod work together in finding and
catching food, or may simply be done for fun.

If a female had calves up until her death, she would leave motherless calves to fend for themselves, cutting down their chances of survival. But a female who stops having calves at a certain age is able to successfully raise her last calf to maturity and ensure her own genes are passed onto another generation. If she then also takes over some of the parenting of her grand-calves as they grow older, she helps her daughter to produce the most calves possible. If an adult female loses her own calves but helps to raise those of her closest kin, she will achieve a modicum of success. Like the adult males, she will be making an investment in the larger gene pool which she shares with her sisters.

As the oldest members of any pod are usually females, they will have greater experience in dealing with the problems of survival. The oceanic environment is very complex. There is a great deal of ocean craft to learn: where to find food and how to catch it; how to travel and stay orientated in a three-dimensional world; which routes are best and what obstacles to avoid; how to deal with shifting currents, temperatures, and depths; how to recognize kin and community and learn the social rules that exist. The longevity and survival skills of the older females increase their importance to the society.

The complex detail of killer whale societies is paralleled only by the societies of elephants and higher primates, again including humans. Although we cannot be certain of its accuracy, we can paint a picture of how a resident killer whale fits into its society through its lifetime.

As a young calf, a killer whale is accepted as part of the social fabric of the pod through its relationship with its mother. It will have open access to all members of the pod, playing with other calves, darting among the adolescents, wrestling with the older males. All pod members will participate in its care, even adult males. In the Pacific Northwest, Norway and Argentina, males of all ages engage in babysitting and educational duties.

During adolescence, relationships with killer whales of its own age develop while most others grow weak. Family alliance is dependent on keeping a close relationship with a 'granny'. With full adulthood, dependency on these 'allo-mothers' declines and direct affiliations with mothers are re-established.

Females have a more integrated place in the society than males, as a result of the dependency on their female kin as they enter the reproductive pool and receive aid in raising offspring. Apart from close affiliations with their mothers, adult males tend to form alliances among themselves. With age, mothers become reproductively inactive and take over support roles.

Distinct sub-groups form through the interplay of a female's age and the number, ages and sex of her offspring. Two scenarios are possible, though in both, adult sons stay with their mothers. An older female with several offspring may stay with her youngest daughter (and her offspring), continuing to function as an 'allo-mother', while her older and more experienced adult daughters (and their offspring) disengage from the larger maternal group and form separate subgroups. However, an older female having only one or two adult daughters may stay closely associated with both, maintaining direct contact throughout her lifetime.

New lineages or pods may form as the older females die out, or as the degree of relatedness between kin begins to thin. Given the long lifespan of killer whales, the formation of new pods is likely to take many decades.

Being more difficult to study, much less is known about transient whale societies. Transient pods are small, averaging three to four whales and only rarely made up of more than six. While these small pods are also composed of the core mother/offspring units, and bonds last through a long adolescence, relationships appear to dissolve upon maturation. Adolescent transient whales appear to emigrate from their birth pod, perhaps traveling alone or forming new pods with other young adults.

These differences from resident whale pods are most probably related to the stricter limits set on the whale's optimal group size by the nature of the primary food resource for transient whales: seals. Transient whale foodstuffs occur in lower densities than the vast schools of salmon which are the predominant prey of resident killer whales. Also, seals or other marine mammals are intelligent and have good hearing. Catching them seems to require small groups which can hunt by stealth. This means that transient pods must remain small, in order to assure that all group members have enough to eat. Both transient and resident killer whales are highly adapted to their habitats ; it is very uncommon to have very separate types of the same species living in the same general region and exploiting very different food resources. Each type has developed a distinctive social organization which is part of their overall adaptation.

The Daily Regime

Blossom lay on her back, whacking her flukes on the water. Slick was still meandering in the kelp bed, letting the long leaves slip over his head, over his dorsal fin and down his back with what seemed erotic delight. In the distance, the rest of their pod was travelling leisurely, lined up abreast of one another. From the charts on our boat, we could see they were swimming over fairly featureless terrain. As they approached the small rise where the 50 foot long bull kelp grew, they slowed and began to mill around. We waited while they took a short break, little calves pushing floating feathers around on their snouts, adults resting at the surface, making soft farting noises from their blow-holes. Up ahead was a narrow channel where the tide rushed through as it changed through its cycles. Soon, the pod moved on. As expected, they began to porpoise through the swirls and eddies, breaching out of the water and becoming thoroughly boisterous, as if they enjoyed the rough playground. We were beginning to be able to predict not only the sequence of their changing behaviors, but what sort of place they would do certain things in.

Personal Diary, June

As long-term studies unfold, we are becoming aware that differences in location affect how populations of killer whales cope with their environment. Every year, new forms of basic behaviors are revealed, showing us how adaptable killer whales can be. Patterns of behavior probably represent cultural mechanisms which have been learned through trial and error and passed down through the generations. If studies in non-American / Canadian waters continue to receive support, they will undoubtedly uncover new variations. Until the results of more studies are available, our picture is simply another summary of killer whales living in British Columbia and Washington State.

Killer whales in the two resident communities organize what they do into a fairly predictable pattern. They travel, searching for schools of fish as they go, and when conditions are right, they begin feeding. After an active hunt and good meal, they settle down for a rest. Upon waking, they break into a round of boisterous socializing before recommencing their travels.

Southern killer whales spend just under half their time foraging, a quarter of it traveling, and resting and socializing about equally the rest of the time. Northern killer whales do things a bit differently: over half of their time is taken up in foraging, and only a small proportion in traveling, but almost a quarter of their time is spent on resting and socializing. Transient killer whales are different again: foraging takes up the bulk of their time, traveling just over an eighth, and play only a tiny fraction. They have yet to be seen resting.

Whether in single groups or multi-pod gangs, traveling killer whales always move at a good pace in a rather determined style, going from place to place in ranked formations. Moving from one feeding area to another, they usually travel across deep, featureless areas. Although they have been observed traveling for up to five and a half hours at one stretch, an average trip lasts around an hour.

Cetaceans do not sleep as other mammals do. It is more like an alert restfulness. Resting killer whales move extremely slowly and methodically in tight clusters, often touching one another, breathing synchronously in shallow rising and falling waves, always silent. Sometimes one or two on the periphery may be on watch, herding other pod members away from obstacles. Resting in stretches of around two hours, killer whales usually choose protected areas away from the main tidal flow. Needing to swim all the time (they would otherwise sink), they occasionally face into a current, using it to stay in one place instead of moving forward.

Socializing killer whales undertake a variety of physical activities and aerial displays, usually in open water areas with underlying kelp-covered sills which generate strong upwelling currents. Playing with inanimate objects, breaching contests (where adults and calves alike come bursting out of the water), belly flops, slapping, rolling and thrashing at the surface, and spyhops (vertical rises on the surface to take in a view from above), are all characteristic play activities. Socializing in multi-pod groups commonly includes sexual interactions. Penile erections in adult and sub-adult males seem to take on an advertizing quality as they are waved around in the air.

Greeting ceremonies are unique to southern killer whales. When they are reunited after a separation of a day or more, each pod forms a row, and hovers at the surface facing the

*Activities, like fluke-waving and playing with inanimate objects,
may help to keep hunting skills fine-tuned.*

Catching seals on sharply pitched beaches in Argentina is a learned technique,
requiring patience and skill. It is passed on to inexperienced young whales through active teaching by adults.
It spite of the dangers, it provides a very rich food source for the whales.

other pod. They then swarm into each other, each individual rubbing and rolling against the other whales. This also happens when the pods awaken after a multi-pod resting session and, just like the social ceremonies in wild dogs and elephants, it appears to re-affirm social bonds.

Beach rubbing is unique to northern whales and constitutes four-and-a-half per cent of their activity. Pods frequently interrupt foraging sessions with visits to a specific 0.5 km section of shoreline on Vancouver Island to rub themselves against two small pebble shelves 3 to 6 m deep. They dive to the bottom and rub for up to a minute at a time. Bouts last up to one-and-a-half hours and are often accompanied by resting and socializing.

When they are foraging and feeding, resident killer whales work in multi-pod groups, usually scattered over a large area in a mixture of small subgroups and individuals and traveling erratically. High-speed swimming with sudden changes in direction, surface lunges and long dive times, and the occasional percussive splash indicate active pursuit or herding of fish. Whereas residents feed in areas of high relief sub-surface topography and along salmon migratory routes, transients feed in shallow protected areas around concentrations of marine mammals. More than any other behavior, the two entirely different foraging strategies of resident and transient killer whales reflect the essential differences between them.

Killer whales are supremely efficient predators. Some might think them tame and playful in captivity, and the name 'killer whale' an unfair one. But in the wild, killer whales do kill, with distinct division of labor and a minimum of fuss. Their reputation as indiscriminate killers has come from a variety of often misinterpreted observations. Famous for preying on other marine mammals, including the largest baleen whales, killer whales actually feed on a diversity of other species: birds, fish, squid, octopus, even sea turtles. But they are not generalized and opportunistic feeders. They specialize on prey which is abundant in their particular area, while having the flexibility to shift their preferences in response to changes in prey abundance.

Like top predators on the African savannah, killer whales live alongside prey species in bouts of neutral coexistence. They mix with pilot whales in the Faroe Islands, and travel with sperm whales and Risso's dolphins off South Africa. Killer whales and minke whales

sometimes feed together in Puget Sound: the minke whales and salmon feeding on small fish fry at the surface and the killer whales hunting the salmon.

Killer whales prey on all marine mammal families, except for river dolphins and manatees. Their seemingly bloodthirsty habits are actually efficient foraging strategies. Young or weak marine mammals are preferred, although killer whales can cooperate to kill healthy adult baleen whales. Most hunts of large whales seem to require groups of more than five killer whales, but success is possible in smaller groups. Sperm whales are rarely killed, and only attacked when with calves.

Seals are hunted by single killer whales and by gangs acting cooperatively. Seal tossing is an effective killing method. Killer whales have been observed regurgitating seal pelts: hitting them out of the water may loosen meat from skin, even tenderizing it.

The most striking display of their predatory powers occurs when killer whales hurl themselves out of the sea, onto a beach, to capture seals. This 'intentional stranding' occurs on gravel beaches in Argentina, and the Crozet Islands in the Indian Ocean. It is a dangerous feeding strategy: it could result in permanent stranding and death. Yet, intentional stranding is such an important skill, that it is passed on from generation to generation. One of the clearest examples of social learning in mammals, intentional stranding is not instinctive: inexperienced individuals must learn it through the observation of, or the active teaching by, experienced individuals.

Off Argentina, it is predominantly adult males who practice intentional stranding. They are the teachers. After capturing but not killing a seal, an adult male pulls it off the shoreline and then releases the now-disabled or disorientated seal. As the adult stands by, younger whales move in to recapture the seal, practicing their own skills.

Off the Crozet Islands, adult females predominantly practice 'intentional stranding' and they are the teachers. Mothers have been observed actively pushing their calf onto the beach, waiting at the ready to rush onto the beach to push a stranded calf back as it learns to imitate the adult behaviors. If a mother is not skilled at intentional stranding, a calf may participate with a more accomplished adult female.

Surplus killing occurs infrequently. It may happen for teaching, play or plain aggression. More

*An Alaskan killer whale takes a shallow dive into a group of fish
herded against the shoreline. While much of killer whale fish-hunting behavior is highly
coordinated, the final capture seems to be made by one individual.*

commonly, killer whales will consume selected parts of some prey, optimizing the most energy-rich titbits.

Fish are as important in the killer whale diet as mammals. Thirty-one species of fish have so far been recorded as killer whale prey. Even where marine mammal predation is common, fish still make up a portion of killer whale stomach contents.

Killer whales use cooperative hunting techniques for fish as well; the degree of cooperation being dependent on the fish's behavior. If the fish live in very tightly grouped schools, cooperative hunting may be more beneficial than if the fish travel solitarily or in loose, small schools.

In Norway, killer whales enter the fjords when groups of herring, a very tightly schooling fish, concentrate for spawning. When they locate a school they begin circling around it, turning sideways and flashing their white bellies to scare the fish and keep them concentrated. This requires a fair degree of organization and cooperation. They must avoid collisions while remaining close enough to keep the herring from escaping, and must also show some degree of restraint: if they all fed at once, the 'carousel' would stop and the fish escape. The killer whales also take turns slapping their massive tail flukes through the school, creating a loud, explosive noise, like the cracking of a whip. Any fish in the path of this tail are stunned or killed and can be picked off at leisure.

The red gills of salmon are sometimes discarded.

In the Pacific Northwest, salmon, which is a moderately schooling fish, is the abundant food source. Killer whales show some degree of cooperation in herding them into concentrations, traveling in a broad, line-abreast flank, splashing with their flukes and flippers, making noise which drives the fish ahead of them. They bunch the salmon against underwater barriers, such as shorelines and seamounts. Once the fish are concentrated, the killer whales feed individually. It has even been found that the resident pods specialize on the largest species of salmon, the chinook or king salmon, even though chinooks are not the most abundant species.

During the early years of research, scientists noted that transients occurred in smaller groups and produced far fewer calves. They were thought to be 'less successful' than resident killer whales. And, because they wandered along the jagged coastline and dead-end bays, they appeared lost in unfamiliar territory.

Now it is clear that the two types are simply specialists. The smaller groups of the transients are the optimal size for capturing marine mammal prey. Their lower reproductive rates may even be related to the numbers of marine mammals available, which are lower compared to the numbers of fish available. It is also clear that the wandering of transients into odd corners is simply their method of exploiting the habitats of seals; while the residents are doing the same by staying in the main channels where the salmon run.

There is an interwoven ecological web between the residents and transients in the Pacific Northwest, which establishes an equilibrium between them. Salmon and seals feed on small fish. Seals also feed on salmon and compete with resident killer whales. Transient killer whales prefer seals. As residents eat more salmon there is less available for the seals, which decrease in number and provide less food for transients. However, fewer salmon allows the numbers of small fish to increase, which provides more food for the seals and eventually more food for the transients.

These complex interactions suggest resident and transient killer whales actually benefit from exploiting the same habitat, and thus their groups may be larger than either type would be on its own.

 Predators throughout the world often specialize on whatever prey is available, but for members of the same species occurring in the same habitat, to exploit different food niches, and to have genetic differences, is very rare.

Killer whales may have lost their reputation as rapacious, frenzied killers,
but this Dall's porpoise knows all too well the efficiency of killer whale predators.
As on the African savannah, this predation probably helps Dall's porpoise
populations by removing weak individuals.

Sound as a Tool

We couldn't see killer whales, but we could hear them through the underwater microphone. Their squeaks, groans and whistles were mild, so we knew they had to be at least five miles away. The sounds became louder as they headed our way. Suddenly, there was a deafening singsong Bree-fftt-whirreep and a cluster of echolocation clicks, making the needle on the tape recorder jump off the scale. Somebody had snuck up and investigated the hydrophone. Slick, in the middle of a group of playful, boisterous killer whales, swept by us in a wave of noise: Bronx squawks blasting out of their blowholes at the surface and wolf-whistles screeching underwater. As they moved off, we ran out of tape and hauled up the hydrophone in frustration. But we could still hear their surface calls, 500 feet away.

Personal Diary, September

In the marine environment, where light, space and distances take on aspects almost unfathomable to terrestrial animals, sound is a most efficient survival tool. All dolphins use streams of echolocation clicks for navigation and locating food and more elaborate calls for communication. The killer whale's intricate social fabric and coordinated movement is maintained through acoustic communication.

The vocal tradition of resident killer whale pods is complex and conveys a wide variety of information, from the location of an individual to the activity and general emotional state of the pod. Communication calls are made up of pure-tone, bird-like whistles and squeaks, grunts and screeching sounds. Calls are either discrete (very distinct and easily separated by ear into characteristic types), variable (calls made randomly and in a great variety of forms) or aberrant (distorted versions of discrete calls).

Discrete calls serve as contact signals – they may be heard at least five miles away – and are used to maintain group cohesion and coordinate movements during travel or foraging. Sung in repetitive series, some are emitted in predictable sequences by individual killer whales. Foraging killer whales emit calls in irregular bursts, with long pauses in-between. One caller can elicit a chorus of responses from others and small groups working alone call less often. Traveling killer whales call at a much higher rate, in excess of 50 per minute, but compact traveling groups, diving and surfacing simultaneously, are sometimes completely silent.

Variable calls are almost exclusively used when killer whales are close together or socializing. They become highly vocal, producing a cacophony of calls; the more social they are, the noisier they become. Very few discrete calls are made but whistles are common, especially during dives. Changes in behavior are always accompanied by a sudden onset of vocal activity involving a wide variety of calls.

Head anatomy is uniquely specialized for sound production and reception.

Young killer whales must learn calls; a rarity among mammals. Vocal learning permits greater flexibility in describing details of social and physical environments, better reflecting changes in both. It also permits the development of a repertoire of calls used as a marker for group identity.

Each resident pod has its own unique repertoire of discrete calls, anywhere from 7 to 17. Some are very distinctive, but others are different in subtle ways. Pods share some calls, sometimes with distinctive versions. These differences make up a local dialect. Pods with dialects which overlap are called 'acoustic clans'. Although they may belong to the same acoustic clan, pods sharing calls may not always travel together.

Killer whales maintain dialects over long periods through strong social and behavioral bonding among pod members. Differences probably occur through the vocal idiosyncrasies of individual killer whales and the accumulation of errors in the copying of calls across

The marine environment is ever-changing and ever-challenging.
Sound is the best orientational tool available to killer whales and smaller dolphins. Their
echolocation gives them a detailed, three-dimensional mental map of the channels
they swim through, as if they were birds soaring over a canyon.

generations. Pod genealogies are probably more accurately traced through common traits in shared calls rather than by assessing which pods associate together.

Compared to resident killer whales, transients are quiet, making calls only during play and after a kill (perhaps to avoid attracting the attention of residents), or as a technique for hunting marine mammals. They commonly produce calls and echolocation clicks together and have small repertoires of discrete calls, from 4 to 7 types. Transient calls are distinct from any produced by resident killer whales. However, transient pods from California, Southeast Alaska and British Columbia share at least one call type, suggesting their acoustic tradition extends over a coastal range of more than 1550 miles (2500 km).

Vision has secondary usefulness.

Norwegian resident killer whale calls are different yet again, especially in structure. At least one complex call from Norway matched an Icelandic call. It was made by killer whales which arrived in the Norwegian fjords much later than other pods and remained socially aloof during their stay. Although the extent of geographical isolation between killer whales observed in Iceland and Norway remains unknown, acoustic research may yet prove a connection.

Even captive killer whales emit the common calls given by their natal pod, remaining unchanged despite long years of separation. They also learn the dialects of their tank companions, who may have come from halfway around the world. This is another clear sign of the important role that is played by learning in the development of killer whale vocalizations.

Groups coordinate their activities using communication calls. Sound can carry in water over many miles, allowing a large area to be searched for food. However, many close-knit groups such as this one travel in complete silence, perhaps relying more on vision to stay in touch.

The many faces of a killer whale's habitat.
We only have a glimpse of the whales' lives at the surface…we are just
beginning to understand how they use the dark ocean depths.

Pods have their own dialects which help them recognize each other. Killer
whales from different parts of the world can learn each other's calls. This complexity of
communication is very rare for mammals, being more common in birds.

Captivity and Conservation

Merlin lay at the surface, barely submerging after each breath, his 6 foot dorsal fin quivering in the golden peach glow of sunset. The rest of J pod floated nearby, all resting before the big push northwards. Fluffy, rose-tinted clouds floated in a piercing blue sky and the glassy waters reflected dark fins and the sky's fire. It seemed the perfect picture of family harmony, a cliché in a nature film. Only a few years previously, J pod had been one of the most heavily harvested groups for live capture operations. We wondered if its missing members were faring well in captivity, and thought of the great difference between these wild creatures and those performing on command in aquariums, knowing the one can never truly depict the other. And we had to ask ourselves if our work was helping this community of killer whales, or was an intrusion causing unknown detriment.

Personal Diary, October

As ambassadors for their species, it cannot be denied that captive killer whales have educated and entertained millions of people annually, helping to change the public's perception of killer whales. People are now so well-informed that the validity of keeping killer whales in aquariums has become a public issue.

The first killer whale ever to be captured was in California. In 1961, a small female floundered into Newport Harbour. She was corralled with small boats and nets and transported to Marineland of the Pacific, in south Los Angeles. She swam around her tank at high speed, eventually rammed into the sides and died the same day. The autopsy revealed she was 25, with very worn teeth, and suffering from acute gastroenteritis and pneumonia. Although a failure, the capture showed it was possible to seize and handle killer whales.

Marineland collectors went to Puget Sound the following year. A female was lassoed, but the line got caught in the propeller. She began vocalizing loudly and a male joined her in attacking the boat; slapping it with their tail flukes. Panicked, the collectors shot at them, eventually killing the female. Needless to say, this temporarily discouraged further attempts.

The next capture was undertaken in the name of art, in 1964. The Vancouver Aquarium intended to kill the killer whale so that a commissioned artist could have accurate measurements to create a realistic sculpture for display. After two months, a small killer whale was harpooned, but not killed. Instead, it was towed 18½ miles (30 km) to Vancouver and placed in a newly-constructed floating pen. Incorrectly named 'Moby Doll', the young male refused to eat for two months. Eventually he began, eating 200 lbs (90 kg) of fish per day. Although he died a month later, Moby Doll proved killer whales could be tamed.

Namu was the next captive, in 1965. Accidentally caught in a fishing net in British Columbia, he was bought by the owner of the Seattle Aquarium for $8000 and towed 435 miles (700 km) to Seattle in a floating pen. Namu lived for a year in captivity, and was seen by thousands of visitors being stroked by people and interacting with them. Namu proved killer whales could be loveable and trained to perform. The terrible reputation of killer whales began to fade and captures for aquarium display began in earnest.

The inland waterways of Washington State and British Columbia were the perfect hunting ground. Killer whales were entrapped in the narrow channels and adjacent bays. Entire groups were encircled and a few of the best individuals selected. The ideal captive was a young male, small enough to transport, but guaranteed to grow into an impressive performer. Over the next 11 years an additional 65 killer whales were captured in the region, although some died during the capture operations.

By the end of 1976, when the last capture was permitted in British Columbia and Washington, 17 captive whales from this region were still alive. Public attitudes had changed dramatically. Killer whales were no longer seen as deadly beasts, but as highly intelligent and loveable symbols of the environmental movement. The public didn't want the whales captured anymore; they wanted them protected. The 'First International Killer Whale Symposium' was held at The Evergreen State College in Olympia, Washington, situated at the southern end of Puget Sound.

Ironically, capture boats encircled a group of six whales just a few miles from Olympia. Hundreds of people converged on the scene and one of the state Governor's assistants witnessed the capture from his sailboat. The state legislature had already been discussing the formation of a killer whale sanctuary in Puget Sound. Because public sympathy was with the whales, it soon became a political issue. The state Attorney General filed suit against the operators.

Small bays, like this one off San Juan Island in Washington State, are typical sites for corralling killer whales during capture operations. Although most of the older whales in this region have been captured and released from such operations, they still freely venture into these bays in pursuit of fish.

While the courts were debating the issue, three of the whales escaped. Eventually, a judge ruled that the remaining whales should be released and invalidated permits for captures in Washington waters.

Although this ended captures in Puget Sound, within a few months, American operators began entrapments off the coast of Iceland. Captures in this part of the Atlantic are now under the jurisdiction of Icelandic operators.

Captive killer whales rate higher than bottlenose dolphins in trainability and reliability. Their highly social nature, natural curiosity, playfulness and fearlessness make it possible for them to adapt well to captivity and training. However, the survival rate in captivity is less than in the wild, and the mortality of captive-born calves has been high. Factors range from possible complications at birth and general poor health (even adults are susceptible to infection and disease in artificial confines), to parental inexperience. In the wild, killer whale females may gain training in calf-rearing from older females, or may get experience by practicing with younger siblings. Females used in breeding programs collected before maturation might simply not know how to be mothers.

Behavioral problems also arise, usually in response to undue stress caused by restraint, strained relations between tank-mates, or poor rapport with trainers. Trainers have sustained injuries from ramming or crushing when leaping performers abort a routine. In 1991, a trainer was hauled around a tank and drowned by an aggravated captive. In 1989, a long-standing conflict between a killer whale from the Pacific Ocean and one from Iceland ended in death, when one rammed the other.

Stress also arises from boredom and living in an artificial environment. It is difficult, if not impossible, to design a tank large enough to suit a 4-ton animal that can travel over 50 miles (80 km) per day in the wild. The complexity of the ocean environment can never be fully reproduced in a concrete tank, no matter how well designed. Most importantly, the social environment of the extended killer whale family is missing in captivity.

Release programs have been considered for captive killer whales, stimulated by increasingly obsolete facilities and successful efforts to send captive bottlenose dolphins back into the wild. 'Keiko', star of the film *Free Willy* brought this issue into dominance at the end of the millennium.

Large males are impressive ambassadors for killer whales. They often travel on the periphery of pods and pass closest to any boats that happen to be in their way. This could be serving a protective role, but may also simply indicate their more independent nature.

Keiko was transferred by the Free Willy Foundation from his rundown tank in Mexico, in 1996, to a state-of-the-art tank in Newport, Oregon, where he lived from January 1996 to September 1998. He was then moved to a floating sea pen in Iceland, the site of his capture at age 2, over 20 years earlier. In late 1999, Keiko was released into a bay roughly 800,000 sq ft (7400 sq m), which was penned off from the open ocean, giving Keiko access to the ocean floor for the first time. The plan is to set Keiko completely free, once he can demonstrate an ability to catch his own food.

In the wild, habitat degradation is probably the greatest problem faced by killer whales. Oil spills and other environmental disasters not only poison killer whales unlucky enough to be caught in them, but they also poison the marine environment, affecting the entire food chain. Depleted fish stocks can lead to increased competition for killer whales with other marine mammals and man.

Fisherman have often clashed with killer whales, some believing they are serious competitors; even today bullets and dynamite are fired at killer whales to protect fisheries. Killer whales have been accused of frightening fish and ruining shoals. They have been considered particularly threatening by Faroese herring and mackerel fishermen, Alaskan blackcod fishermen, and salmon fishermen in British Columbia and Washington State. In 1956, Icelandic fishermen in the Greenland halibut fisheries became so alarmed that the US Navy was requested to rid the coastal waters of killer whales.

Having learned to exploit boats, killer whales wait nearby, snatching fish falling out of nets or eating netted fish and tearing nets, costing up to 25,000 dollars apiece, in the process. They also take fish off hooked lines, removing the body and leaving the head containing the hook. In Prince William Sound, Alaska, it is only a few specific pods that have specialized in this feeding method, and even then, their 'theft' only amounts to 3 per cent of the fishery's value. Yet the exploitation is mutual: salmon boats set nets in the path of foraging killer whales, and mackerel boats track them on ships' sonar to locate schooling fish.

Killer whales, especially those populations which feed on marine mammals, are already registering high levels of industrial toxins. The world's arsenal of toxic chemicals eventually ends up in the marine environment, deposited directly from ships, nearshore drainage, and rivers,

The rubbing rocks at Robson Bight are part of an ecological reserve for Canadian killer whales.

where they not only directly affect organisms, but are taken up by plants and into the food chain. Permanently stored in fatty tissues, toxins become more and more concentrated as predator eats prey. Top predators end up with the jackpot. A particularly cruel pattern of toxin concentration also occurs between mother and calf. Unborn calves absorb toxins through the bloodstream and young calves feed on mothers' polluted, yet rich, fatty milk – the equivalent of double cream. Even before they start hunting on their own, they may have high toxin concentrations.

The worldwide distribution of killer whales puts them in contact with, and at risk from, ever-increasing shipping traffic, accidental oil spills and contamination from other pollutants. After the Exxon Valdez oil spill in Prince William Sound, Alaska, killer whales resident to that area had toxin levels (specifically, polychlorinated biphenyls, or PCBs) three times higher than that which has been shown to cause immune system deficiencies in captive seals. One pod of 25 whales has never been seen again after last being observed swimming directly through the oil slick. Given their long-term residency of the region, they are currently presumed dead.

Habitats also need protection.

Increased shipping also means increased noise which is filling the world's oceans with 'noise pollution'. The sensitive hearing and complex communication of killer whales can be drowned out by this noise, reducing their hunting abilities both in terms of passively detecting potential prey and also in their ability to acoustically coordinate their cooperative hunting behaviors.

The impact of removing animals from a population is unknown. In the Pacific Northwest, the differences between the northern and southern resident communities in age and sex structure and reproductive rates are the result of early capture operations which removed prime individuals from the population. Yet, until captive breeding programs became more successful, captures will probably continue. No one can tell whether killer whales would be driven from their home territories or their social fabric destroyed if removals continue. And we have yet to assess other, seemingly benign human activities which impact wild killer whales. The increasingly popular pastime of boat-based whale-watching activities may have long-term effects equally detrimental: increased stress from constant boat traffic, noise disturbance, and habitat degradation, to name just a few. Research activities also lie in this balance between intrusion and consideration.

The combination of long lives, slow maturation rates, variable birth rates and very slow population growth implies extremely slow recovery of any affected stock, taking several generations. Yet, because killer whales are not recognized as being endangered, and are still not considered particularly important natural resources in countries other than Canada and the United States, they receive no special protective status or legislation.

The US Marine Mammal Protection Act of 1972 has numerous provisions for protecting marine mammals, ranging from banning all import/export of marine mammal products, to the protection of habitat and prosecution for harassment. Researchers, film-makers, and whale-watching activities are required to obtain a permit from the US Marine Mammal Commission to conduct activities closer than 110 yards (100 m); violation of this order leads to prosecution and a fine of up to $10,000. The government of the United States has also designated various marine habitats as protected marine sanctuaries, many of which are important to killer whales. Similarly, Canada created the Robson Bight-Michael Bigg Ecological Reserve on Vancouver Island, to protect the all-important rubbing rocks of the northern resident killer whale community. This area had been under threat by logging operations during the 1970s and 1980s. Pressure from scientists, environmental groups and the public caused the government of British Columbia to take action.

This sort of public action, from the people who know and care about killer whales, and the delicate balance of their marine habitat, is the best protection for killer whales. Hopefully, as we continue to sort the myths from the realities about killer whales, we will only gain a greater, richer appreciation for them as one of Nature's most powerful representatives. Without killer whales, some of the earth's magic would be lost.

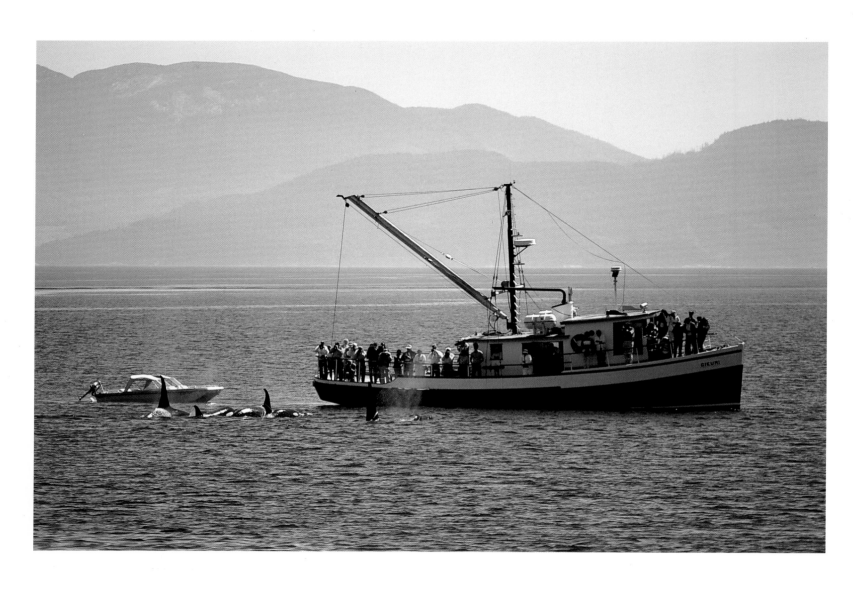

Boat-based whale-watching should be undertaken through sanctioned excursions. Crews on experienced expeditions are conscientious towards cetaceans well-being. The recommended code of conduct for encountering cetaceans follows common sense. Never block their passage, approach no closer than 110 yds (100 m) and never from directly in front. Remain to the side or behind the group and keep to its speed without sudden accelerations. Never swim near or attempt to touch cetaceans. Violation of these guidelines constitutes harassment and can cause discomfort, even distress. It also turns whale-watching into an artificial experience, not much different from seeing them on television or in an aquarium.

Killer Whale Facts

	Female	Male
Common name	Killer Whale or Orca	
Scientific name	*Orcinus orca*	
Body Measurements	Female	Male
Maximum Adult Length	9.30 yds (8.5 m)	10.61 yds (9.7 m)
Average Adult Length	6.34 yds (5.8 m)	7.33 yds (6.7 m)
Average Adult Weight	6064 lbs (2750 kg)	8820 lbs (4000 kg)
Dorsal Fin Height	1 yd (1 m)	2 yds (1.8 m)
Length at birth	2.3 yds (2.1 m)	2.3 yds (2.1 m)
Gestation (months)	15	
Age at maturity	15	21
Longevity (years)	80	50-60

Longevity – The maximum longevity for female killer whales is around 80 years old. Maximum longevity for males is shorter, probably around 50 or 60 years.

Distribution – Killer whales are distributed throughout all oceans and may be seen at all latitudes. However, the majority of concentrations are in the cooler, continental shelf waters of mid to high-latitudes.

Where to see Killer Whales

Killer whales, with their tall dorsal fins and striking markings, often in large, active groups, are some of the most impressive cetaceans to see in the wild. There is a certain skill to being in the right place at the right time. In the UK, the Hebrides, Orkney and Shetland Islands, off the coast of Scotland, are frequented by small groups of killer whales during summer and fall. The inland marine waters of Washington State and British Columbia are the best location to find killer whales from shore or boat, from July to September. San Juan Island, in northern Washington boasts America's only official whale-watching park where killer whales pass just off the rocks. The Robson Bight-Michael Bigg Ecological Reserve on Vancouver Island is the Canadian equivalent.

Index

Biographical Note

Sara L Heimlich and James R Boran have been studying cetaceans since the mid 1970s. **Sara** provided the first evidence suggesting the matrilineal social organization in killer whales, at the first Orca Symposium in the 1980s, in Seattle, Washington. Her Master's thesis provided one of the early quantitative descriptions of killer whale social organization and long-term social bonds. She has worked on a variety of cetacean research projects, including a ground-breaking study on short-finned pilot whales in the Canary Islands, where she was co-principal investigator with James Boran. She is based in the USA.

James holds a B. A. from the Evergreen State College, Olympia, WA, USA, an M.Sc. in Marine Science from San Jose State University, CA, USA, and a Ph.D. from the University of Cambridge. He has worked on a wide variety of original research projects on the behavioural and social ecology of cetaceans, primarily killer whales and short-finned pilot whales. He is currently a Graduate Tutor at the University of Manchester Institute of Science and Technology (UMIST) in Manchester, England, where he lives with his partner, Dr. M. J. Rosen.

Recommended Reading

The most comprehensive reports on the long-term studies on killer whales in Washington and British Columbia have been published in a Report of the International Whaling Commission, Special Issue No.12, Individual Recognition of Cetaceans 1980. Earlier studies were collected in the volume *The Behavioral Biology of Killer Whales*, edited by Barbara Kirkevold & Joan Lockard, A. R. Liss, 1986. The best popular account of killer whales is Erich Hoyt's *Orca: The Whales Called Killer*, Camden House, Ontario, Canada, 1984. Guides to areas for seeing killer whales are in *The Whale Watcher's Handbook* by Erich Hoyt, Doubleday and Co., Inc., Garden City, N.Y., 1984, and *Where the Whales Are* by Patricia Corgan, The Globe Pequot Press, Chester, CT. 1991.